A
Shame
To
Miss

I

Poetry collections by Anne Fine published by Corgi Books:
A SHAME TO MISS . . . 1
A SHAME TO MISS . . . 2
A SHAME TO MISS . . . 3

Published by Doubleday for older readers:

UP ON CLOUD NINE
'A real treat for the many fans of the Children's Laureate; a
highly enjoyable novel that is characteristically funny, clever
and moving'
Financial Times

Other books by Anne Fine for older readers:
THE SUMMER-HOUSE LOON
THE OTHER DARKER NED
THE STONE MENAGERIE
ROUND BEHIND THE ICEHOUSE
THE GRANNY PROJECT
MADAME DOUBTFIRE
GOGGLE-EYES
THE BOOK OF THE BANSHEE
FLOUR BABIES
STEP BY WICKED STEP
THE TULIP TOUCH

Published by Doubleday/Yearling for junior readers:

CHARM SCHOOL
'A funny read which pre-teens should latch on to' *Children's
Bookseller*

BAD DREAMS
'A beautifully plotted, well-told mix of fantasy thriller and
closely observed school drama' *Daily Telegraph*

www.annefine.co.uk

A Shame To Miss 1

SELECTED BY

ANNE FINE

Corgi Books

A SHAME TO MISS . . . 1
A CORGI BOOK 0 552 548677

Published in Great Britain by Corgi Books,
an imprint of Random House Children's Books

This edition published 2002

1 3 5 7 9 10 8 6 4 2

Compilation, introduction and notes copyright © Anne Fine, 2002
Borders and decorations © Vanessa Card, 2002

The right of Anne Fine to be identified as the compiler of this work has been
asserted in accordance with the Copyright, Designs and Patents Act 1988

The Acknowledgements on page 151 constitute an extension of this
copyright notice.

Papers used by Random House Children's Books are natural, recyclable
products made from wood grown in sustainable forests. The manufacturing
processes conform to the environmental regulations of the country of origin.

Set in Palatino

Corgi Books are published by Random House Children's Books,
61–63 Uxbridge Road, London W5 5SA,
a division of The Random House Group Ltd,
in Australia by Random House Australia (Pty) Ltd,
20 Alfred Street, Milsons Point, Sydney, NSW 2061, Australia,
in New Zealand by Random House New Zealand Ltd,
18 Poland Road, Glenfield, Auckland 10, New Zealand,
and in South Africa by Random House (Pty) Ltd,
Endulini, 5A Jubilee Road, Parktown 2193, South Africa.

THE RANDOM HOUSE GROUP Limited Reg. No. 954009

www.kidsatrandomhouse.co.uk

A CIP catalogue record for this book is available from the British Library.

Typeset by SX Composing DTP, Rayleigh, Essex
Printed and bound in Great Britain by
Bookmarque Ltd, Croydon, Surrey

Contents

Introduction

Many young people come to poetry through someone older with a passion for it. Others have to manage by themselves, and it can be difficult.

I still remember exactly why it was I didn't 'get' lots of the poems I came across. I remember which words I didn't understand, and even which bits I couldn't follow because of things no one had told me.

I've chosen these particular poems because, if I were your mother or teacher, these are the ones I really wouldn't want you to miss. And I've tried to explain everything you need to know to enjoy them first time.

Anne Fine

P.S. Back in school I adored writing, and teachers often used poems as a jumping-off

point. It made it so easy to think of something to get started.

So sometimes, under the poem, I've told you about the sort of things we did, in case you're stuck in a caravan during a wet week in Weston-super-Mare and want to bribe your parents into paying you for having a go at the quiet ones.

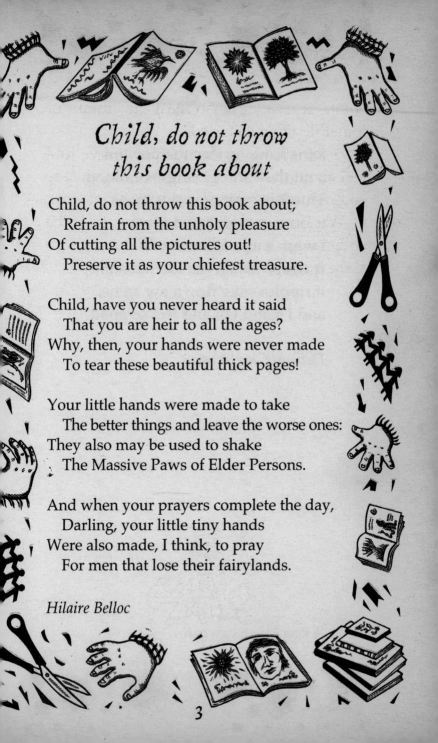

Child, do not throw
this book about

Child, do not throw this book about;
    Refrain from the unholy pleasure
Of cutting all the pictures out!
    Preserve it as your chiefest treasure.

Child, have you never heard it said
    That you are heir to all the ages?
Why, then, your hands were never made
    To tear these beautiful thick pages!

Your little hands were made to take
    The better things and leave the worse ones:
They also may be used to shake
    The Massive Paws of Elder Persons.

And when your prayers complete the day,
    Darling, your little tiny hands
Were also made, I think, to pray
    For men that lose their fairylands.

Hilaire Belloc

My Sari

Saris hang on the washing line:
a rainbow in our neighbourhood.
This little orange one is mine,
it has a mango leaf design.
I wear it as a Rani would.
It wraps round me like sunshine,
it ripples silky down my spine,
and I stand tall and feel so good.

Debjani Chatterjee

A Rani is an Indian queen.

The Ugly Child

I heard them say I'm ugly.
I hoped it wasn't true.
I looked into the mirror
To get a better view,
And certainly my face seemed
Uninteresting and sad.
I *wish* that either it was good
Or else just very bad.

My eyes are green, my hair is straight,
My ears stick out, my nose
Has freckles on it all the year,
I'm skinny as a hose.
If only I could look as I
Imagine I might be.
Oh, all the crowds would turn and bow.
They don't – because I'm me.

Elizabeth Jennings

'My Heart Is Broken,'
Cried the Owl

'My heart is broken,' cried the Owl
   and the Moon answered: 'No.
Mop up your tears with a towel
Let no broken-hearted fowl
Rend the night with hoot and howl.
Mop up your tears with a towel.
   I am ashamed of you.'

The Owl repeated: 'Too whit too whoo'
   up at the angry Moon.
'Too whit too whoo, too whit too whoo.
It is all very well for you
Sitting up in the starry sky
With the Lion and Seven Sisters by,
But down here in the haunted tree
There is no one else but me.
I can feel my poor heart groan
Because' – he sobbed – 'I'm so alone.'
The Owl wept in his bitter grief
And wiped his eye upon a leaf.

'Come, Owl. Come, Owl,' the Moon replied.
   'It's not as bad as that.
Lift up your head and you will find
Stars all around you and your kind.
No Owl should ever quite despair
As long as I shine in the air.
Come, here's a slightly drier towel.
Cry Cheerio Cheerio, you old Owl.'

George Barker

'Fowl' is another word for bird, 'rend' means tear up,
and the Lion and Seven Sisters are star patterns.

Mouth Open,
Story Jump Out

Mouth open
story jump out

I tell you me secret
you let it out

Besides,
the secret I tell you
wasn't even true
so you can shout
till you blue

So boo
mouth open
story jump out

But I don't care
if the world hear
shout it out
Mouth open
story jump out.

John Agard

A Frosty Night

'Alice, dear, what ails you,
Dazed and lost and shaken?
Has the chill night numbed you?
Is it fright you have taken?'

'Mother, I am very well,
I was never better.
Mother do not hold me so,
Let me write my letter.'

'Sweet my dear, what ails you?'
'No, but I am well,
The night was cold and frosty –
There's no more to tell.'

'Ay the night was frosty,
Coldly gaped the moon,
Yet the birds seemed twittering
Through green boughs of June.

'Soft and thick the snow lay,
Stars danced in the sky –
Not all the lambs of May-day
Skip so bold and high.

'Your feet were dancing, Alice.
Seemed to dance on air,
You looked a ghost or angel
In the star-light there.

'Your eyes were frosted starlight;
Your heart, fire and snow.
Who was it said, "I love you"?'
'Mother, let me go!'

Robert Graves

*This sets us wondering what happened before
the poem began. You might try deciding what
that was, then write Alice's letter for her.*

A Was an Archer

A was an Archer, who shot at a frog.
B was a Butcher, who had a great dog.
C was a Captain, all covered with lace.
D was a Dunce, with a very sad face.
E was an Esquire, with pride on his brow.
F was a Farmer, who followed the plough.
G was a Gamester, who had but ill luck.
H was a Hunter, who hunted a buck.
I was an Innkeeper, who loved to bowse.
J was a Joiner, who built up a house.
K was a King, so mighty and grand,
L was a Lady, who had a white hand.
M was a Miser, who hoarded his gold.
N was a Nobleman, gallant and bold.
O was an Oysterman, who went about town.
P was a Parson, who wore a black gown.
Q was a Quack, with a wonderful pill.
R was a Robber, who wanted to kill.
S was a Sailor, who spent all he got.
T was a Tinker, who mended a pot.
U was a Usurer, a miserable elf.

V was a Vintner, who drank all himself.
W was a Watchman, who guarded the door.
X was Expensive, and so became poor.
Y was a Youth, that did not love school.
Z was a Zany, a poor harmless fool.

Traditional

A gamester is a gambler.
Bowsing is having a merry, drunken time.
A parson is a vicar.
A quack makes money selling pretend medicines. (Never
call your doctor a quack if you want to stay healthy.)
A usurer lends out money but demands a whole lot more
back later.
Vintners make wine.

Cargoes

Quinquireme of Nineveh from distant
   Ophir
Rowing home to haven in sunny Palestine,
With a cargo of ivory
And apes and peacocks,
Sandalwood, cedarwood, and sweet white
   wine.

Stately Spanish galleon coming from the
   Isthmus,
Dipping through the tropics by the palm-
   grove shores,
With a cargo of diamonds,
Emeralds, amethysts,
Topazes, and cinnamon, and gold moidores.

Dirty British coaster with a salt-caked
   smoke-stack,
Butting through the Channel in the mad
   March days,
With a cargo of Tyne coal,
Road-rails, pig-lead,
Firewood, ironware, and cheap tin trays.

John Masefield

*Three very different ships with three very different loads.
It's going to take an atlas and a dictionary to be
absolutely sure of every place and every word in this one.*

Dirge for a Bad Boy

Richard has been sent to bed:
Let a solemn dirge be said.
Sent to bed before his time,
Sentenced for a nursery crime.
Draw down the blinds in every room
And fill the dismal house with gloom.
Richard has been sent to bed:
Let a solemn dirge be said.

Tell the cat and kitten they
Must cease from their unseemly play.
Stop the telephone from ringing;
Stop the kettle from its singing.
And hark, is that the Hoover's hum?
Let the Hoover too be dumb.
Richard has been sent to bed:
Let a solemn dirge be said.

Turn off, turn off, the central heat,
And let the cold creep round our feet.
Put out the fire and let it die
Underneath that juicy pie,
That we may eat (if eat we must)
Cold apple and a colder crust.
Richard has been sent to bed:
Let a solemn dirge be said.

And when the time has come for all
To follow through the darkened hall,
Let every sound of mirth be banned –
Take each a candle in his hand,
And winding up the stairway slow
In melancholy order go,
While this solemn dirge is said
For a poor sinner in his bed.

E. V. Rieu

*A dirge is a funeral song. We'd have been asked to write
Richard's side of the story, and mine would definitely
have begun something like: 'It certainly wasn't* my
fault!'

Napoleon Bonaparte and his French armies were the great enemy of Britain until the Battle of Waterloo in 1815.

No one would win a Good Parenting award singing a lullaby like the poem on the next page. But we really enjoyed writing our own horrible cradle songs. (If you try it, please don't sing the results to anyone younger than six!)

Giant Bonaparte

Baby, baby, naughty baby,
Hush, you squalling thing, I say.
Peace this moment, peace, or maybe
Bonaparte will pass this way.

Baby, baby, he's a giant,
Tall and black as Rouen steeple,
And he breakfasts, dines, rely on't,
Every day on naughty people.

Baby, baby, if he hears you,
As he gallops past the house,
Limb from limb at once he'll tear you,
Just as pussy tears a mouse.

And he'll beat you, beat you, beat you,
And he'll beat you all to pap,
And he'll eat you, eat you, eat you,
Every morsel snap, snap, snap.

Traditional

Love Without Hope

Love without hope, as when the young
   bird-catcher
Swept off his tall hat to the Squire's own
   daughter,
So let the imprisoned larks escape and fly
Singing about her head, as she rode by.

Robert Graves

*To save carrying cages, bird-catchers kept what they'd
already caught that day safely under very high hats till
they got home.*

Fog in November

Fog in November, trees have no heads.
Streams only sound, walls suddenly stop
Half-way up hills, the ghost of a man spreads
Dung on dead fields for next year's crop.
I cannot see my hand before my face,
My body does not seem to be my own,
The world becomes a far-off, foreign place,
People are strangers, houses silent, unknown.

Leonard Clark

Sea Timeless Song

Hurricane come
and hurricane go
but sea . . . sea timeless
sea timeless
sea timeless
sea timeless
sea timeless

Hibiscus bloom
then dry-wither so
but sea . . . sea timeless
sea timeless
sea timeless
sea timeless
sea timeless

Tourist come
and tourist go
but sea . . . sea timeless
    sea timeless
    sea timeless
    sea timeless
    sea timeless

Grace Nichols

*Hibiscus is the sort of floppy bright flower you want to
wear in your hair. What I so love about this is the
simple, graceful way the poet conjures the sound of
waves tirelessly reaching shore.*

This next is the saddest poem. Partly that someone so young, away at boarding school, would lose his father and have to be told by his headmaster, however kind.

And partly that the bullies could be making the boy's life such a misery that his feelings about his father's death end up coming second.

The Lesson

'Your father's gone,' my bald headmaster
   said.
His shiny dome and brown tobacco jar
Splintered at once in tears. It wasn't grief.
I cried for knowledge which was bitterer
Than any grief. For there and then I knew
That grief has uses – that a father dead
Could bind the bully's fist a week or two;
And then I cried for shame, then for relief.

I was a month past ten when I learnt this:
I still remember how the noise was stilled
In school-assembly when my grief came in.
Some goldfish in a bowl quietly sculled
Around their shining prison on its shelf.
They were indifferent. All the other eyes
Were turned towards me. Somewhere in
   myself
Pride like a goldfish flashed a sudden fin.

Edward Lucie-Smith

25

Gust Becos I Cud Not Spel

Gust becos I cud not spel
It did not mean I was daft
When the boys in school red my riting
Some of them laffed.

But now I am the dictater
They have to rite like me
Utherwise they cannot pas
Ther GCSE

Some of the girls wer ok
But those who laffed a lot
Have al bean rownded up
And hav recintly bean shot

The teecher who corrected my speling
As not been shot at al
But four the last fifteen howers
As bean standing up against a wal

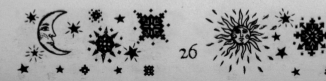

He has to stand ther until he can spel
Figgymisgrugifooniyn the rite way
I think he will stand ther forever
I just inventid it today

Brian Patten

*Twins I know got so bored they had a competition
translating this into proper spelling. Then they fell out
over the marking and one blacked the other's eye.*

Mirrors

Mirrors have haunted me
Since I was four –
Mirrors to be stared into, mirrors on the door,
Mirrors in the fairground, mirrors in the sea:
Each and every one of them
Has haunted me.

Windows in the buses,
Puddles in the street –
Each can be a mirror. You can splash your feet,
See your face exploding, watch the world
    go 'Puff'.
Mirrors shows us what we are,
Yet it's not enough.

Elizabeth Jennings

*Staring into your own eyes in a mirror quickly turns
creepy. How about writing a really chilling tale that
starts with someone idly doing that?*

The Reverend Sabine
Baring-Gould

The Reverend Sabine Baring-Gould,
    Rector (sometime) at Lew,
Once at a Christmas party asked,
    'Whose pretty child are you?'

(The Rector's family was long,
    His memory was poor,
And as to who was who had grown
    Increasingly unsure.)

At this, the infant on the stair
    Most sorrowfully sighed.
'Whose pretty little girl am I?
    Why, *yours*, papa!' she cried.

Charles Causley

*This happens. Two professors I knew exchanged children
by mistake after a chat in the street. (You could describe
what happened when they all got home.)*

29

From *Macbeth*
(Act IV, Scene i)

Round about the cauldron go;
In the poisoned entrails throw.
Toad, that under cold stone
Days and nights has thirty-one
Sweltered venom sleeping got
Boil thou first i' th' charmed pot!

Double, double toil and trouble;
Fire burn and cauldron bubble.
Fillet of a fenny snake,
In the cauldron boil and bake;
Eye of newt, and toe of frog,
Wool of bat, and tongue of dog,
Adder's fork, and blind-worm's sting,
Lizard's leg, and howlet's wing.
For a charm of powerful trouble,
Like a hell-broth, boil and bubble.

Double, double toil and trouble;
Fire burn and cauldron bubble.
Cool it with a baboon's blood,
Then the charm is firm and good.

William Shakespeare

*I remember we half-copied this poem, putting in our own
ingredients. It was interesting how the class split into a
few wimps who chose nice things and had clearly decided
to do white magic, and all the rest, like me, who went
straight for things even more unpleasant than
Shakespeare's.*

The Doll's House

Open the doors
and let your little fat pinkies
prowl through these rooms.

There is no cellar
with dark stairs
to frighten the children.

It is a house
with no roots at all.
Come into the hall

and tap the barometer
that hangs on the wall.
It will neither rise nor fall.

In the kitchen
you will touch
the little red paper fire

that glows in the range,
then put your finger
to your mouth

and make a show
of being burned.
They all do.

And you may,
if you will,
mumble my wooden food.

Upstairs, in the bedroom,
you will not fail
to lift up the pretty valance

and find
to your feigned
and loud delight

that there is indeed
a guzunder there.
For this is an old house

and as its ways
are not your ways,
improprieties

are of no account.
But when you find me
and try to lift me,

as I know you will,
you will find
that someone –

oh, it was years ago –
thought fit to stitch me
into my chair.

Neil Curry

*This poem has always struck me as horribly sinister. The
tiny doll telling you all this doesn't sound much of a
child-lover. There again, being stitched to a chair for a
lifetime wouldn't be good for anyone's personality.*

*A 'guzunder' is a potty (it 'goes under' the bed). A
'valance' is the frill round a bed. 'Improprieties' means
poor manners.*

The Unexplorer

There was a road ran past our house
Too lovely to explore.
I asked my mother once – she said
That if you followed where it led
It brought you to the milk-man's door.
(That's why I have not travelled more.)

Edna St Vincent Millay

*This happened to me, too. A magical, winding path
between bushes behind my grandparents' house led to –
everyone's dustbins!*

In the days before engines, no ship could get home till the winds were right, so wives on shore sang plenty of lullabies like this next poem.

I think it's better sung than spoken, so forget the baby and make up a tune.

Sweet and Low

Sweet and low, sweet and low,
   Wind of the western sea,
Low, low, breathe and blow,
   Wind of the western sea!
Over the rolling waters go,
Come from the dying moon, and blow,
   Blow him again to me;
While my little one, while my pretty one,
     sleeps.

Sleep and rest, sleep and rest,
   Father will come to thee soon;
Rest, rest, on mother's breast,
   Father will come to thee soon;
Father will come to his babe in the
     nest,
Silver sails all out of the west
    Under the silver moon:
Sleep, my little one, sleep, my pretty
     one, sleep.

Alfred, Lord Tennyson

I Hate Poems

I hate poems.
I hate poems because
They're always about custard
And teachers who are not like my teachers
And putting your finger up your nose
And monsters in the classroom
And children who are rough and being sick.

I hate poems.
I hate poets who come and shout
Their words and batter me with language
I do not use in accents I can't understand.

I hate poems.
Because they shut the windows in my mind
With their custard and their fingers
And their shouting.
When the poets come I look
Out of the windows to the gardens opposite
And watch the daffodils dancing.

Susan Hamlyn

You'll know exactly *the sorts of poems she means.*

Hist   Whist

hist   whist
little ghostthings
tip-toe
twinkle-toe

little twitchy
witches and tingling
goblins
hob-a-nob   hob-a-nob

little hoppy happy
toad in tweeds
tweeds
little itchy mousies

with scuttling
eyes   rustle and run   and
hidehidehide
whisk

whisk   look out for the old woman
with the wart on her nose
what she'll do to yer
nobody knows

for she knows the devil   ooch
the devil   ouch
the devil
ach   the great

green
dancing
devil
devil

devil
devil

     wheeEEE

E. E. Cummings

*If it weren't so short, this would practically be a stage
play. If you read it aloud, don't forget to start soft and
creepy, then turn threatening, then go for the big finale.
Make 'em* jump.

The Listeners

'Is there anybody there?' said the Traveller,
  Knocking on the moonlit door;
And his horse in the silence champed the
    grasses
  Of the forest's ferny floor:
And a bird flew up out of the turret,
  Above the Traveller's head:
And he smote upon the door a second time;
  'Is there anybody there?' he said.
But no one descended to the Traveller;
  No head from the leaf-fringed sill
Leaned over and looked into his grey eyes,
  Where he stood perplexed and still.
But only a host of phantom listeners
  That dwelt in the lone house then
Stood listening in the quiet of the moonlight
  To that voice from the world of men:
Stood thronging the faint moonbeams on
    the dark stair,
  That goes down to the empty hall,
Hearkening in an air stirred and shaken
  By the lonely Traveller's call.

And he felt in his heart their strangeness,
    Their stillness answering his cry,
While his horse moved, cropping the dark
        turf,
    'Neath the starred and leafy sky;
For he suddenly smote on the door, even
    Louder, and lifted his head: –
'Tell them I came, and no one answered,
    That I kept my word,' he said.
Never the least stir made the listeners,
    Though every word he spake
Fell echoing through the shadowiness of
        the still house
    From the one man left awake:
Ay, they heard his foot upon the stirrup,
    And the sound of iron on stone,
And how the silence surged softly backward,
    When the plunging hoofs were gone.

Walter de la Mare

The Eagle

He clasps the crag with crooked hands;
Close to the sun in lonely lands,
Ring'd with the azure world, he stands.
The wrinkled sea beneath him crawls;
He watches from his mountain walls,
And like a thunderbolt he falls.

Alfred, Lord Tennyson

*Azure is blue. The wrinkling on the sea is the waves seen
from a great height, before the eagle folds his wings to
drop on his prey even faster.*

The Yak

As a friend to the children, commend me
   the Yak.
  You will find it exactly the thing:
It will carry and fetch, you can ride on its
   back,
  Or lead it about with a string.

The Tartar who dwells on the plains of Thibet
  (A desolate region of snow)
Has for centuries made it a nursery pet,
  And surely the Tartar should know!

Then tell your parents where the Yak can be
   got,
  And if he is awfully rich
He will buy you the creature – or else he
   will *not*.
  (I cannot be positive which.)

Hilaire Belloc

Tartars were about as fierce a tribespeople as you could
find, and a yak – a hairy ox – must weigh half a tonne.

She Lies by the Island
of Spices and Zephyrs

She lies by the Island of Spices and Zephyrs
where the monkeys play hide and seek up
   in old trees
and the humming-birds balance all day on
   a single
blade of tall grass as it sways in the breeze.

There the gold fish blow bubbles among
   water lilies
simply to pass the time of the day
and high on the mountain the summer
   cloud lingers
rather than pass on its heavenly way.

A zephyr is a soft wind. A basilisk was a magic serpent
that could kill you just by looking at you. The f'castle
(fo'c'sle) or forecastle is in the bow or front of a ship.

She lies there and roses climb out of her
    portholes,
the juniper trails from her f'castle down.
At her figurehead glitters the eye of the
    basilisk
like the sea-green jewel of a gold crown.

She lies there, rock riven, her mizzen mast
    shattered
and the seaweeds garb her all over in green.
Who was she? Who knows? Who knows?
    No one.
The name on her side will never be seen.

George Barker

*If I had to write about how the shipwreck happened, I
know I'd have wasted half the time deciding on the ship's
name.*

Once Upon a Time

Once Upon a Time,
Once Upon a Time!
Everything that happened, happened
Once Upon a Time!

Lovely ladies wed with beasts,
Tablecloths provided feasts
    When addressed in rhyme,
Magic fish could not refuse
Anything you cared to choose,
Kitchenmaids wore crystal shoes,
    Once Upon a Time!

Little girls in scarlet hoods
Talked with wolves and things in woods,
    Bullfrogs in the slime
Lived enchanted in their fen
Till Kings' Daughters stooped again,
Kissed, and changed them into men,
    Once Upon a Time!

Once Upon a Time,
Once Upon a Time!
Younger Sons were in their glory,
And the end of every story
    Was a wedding chime;
Girls made ladders of their tresses,
Magic nuts held fairy dresses,
Princes wed the right Princesses,
    Once Upon a Time!

What has happened? Nothing happens!
    Life is past its prime,
Everything that happened, happened
    Once Upon a Time.

Eleanor Farjeon

fen = marshy land
tresses = hair
past its prime = gone off, turned grey and dull

49

Big Hole

My best friend Jenny Colquhoun has
    moved on.
She's gone to live in a posher part of town.
She left a big hole; an empty space next to
    my desk.
My hands hold themselves on the way to
    school.

But see in her new house she has a dining
    room,
a TV room – imagine a room just for
    watching! –
and her own bedroom. I stayed the night;
got lost on my way back from the bathroom.

I was there the day before her ninth birthday.
I was the special friend from the old school.
But when her new friends came they stared
till I thought I should check the mirror, as if

I had a big hole in my tights. 'What did *you*
get Jenny for her birthday?' *'Anne of Green
Gables'*
I said, burning under the wrong dress,
wanting the thick carpet to swallow me up.

'Have you always been that colour?' says
the one
with the freckles. And a giggle spreads
from room
to room till Jenny's beautiful red-haired
mother
saves me: *'Anne of Green Gables*? A wonderful
book.'

Jackie Kay

*If your best friend won the Lottery and moved up in the
world, do you suppose you would enjoy the visit? (If you
enjoy writing quarrels, you could suppose it was you
who had lent her the money to buy her lottery ticket, and
she wouldn't share the winnings.)*

The Song of Shadows

Sweep thy faint strings, Musician,
With thy long lean hand.
Downward the starry tapers burn,
Sinks soft the waning sand.
The old hound whimpers, couched in sleep;
The embers smoulder low:
Across the wall the shadows
  Come and go.

Sweep softly thy strings, Musician,
The minutes mount to hours.
Frost on the windless casement weaves
A labyrinth of flowers.
Ghosts linger in the darkening air,
Hearken at the open door;
Music hath called them, dreaming,
  Home once more.

Walter de la Mare

The Magic Box

I will put in the box

the swish of a silk sari on a summer night,
fire from the nostrils of a Chinese dragon,
the tip of a tongue touching a tooth.

I will put in the box

a snowman with a rumbling belly,
a sip of the bluest water from Lake Lucerne,
a leaping spark from an electric fish.

I will put in the box

three violet wishes spoken in Gujarati,
the last joke of an ancient uncle
and the first smile of a baby.

I will put in the box

a fifth season and a black sun,
a cowboy on a broomstick
and a witch on a white horse.

My box is fashioned from ice and gold and
    steel,
with stars on the lid and secrets in the corners.
Its hinges are the toe joints
of dinosaurs.

I shall surf on my box
on the great high-rolling breaks of the wild
    Atlantic,
then wash ashore on a yellow beach
the colour of the sun.

Kit Wright

*Lots of people copy out the 'I will put in the box' lines
and then choose their own things to make up their own
poem.*

Choosing a Name

I have got a new-born sister;
I was nigh the first that kissed her.
When the nursing woman brought her
To papa, his infant daughter,
How papa's dear eyes did glisten! –
She will shortly be to christen:
And papa has made the offer,
I shall have the naming of her.

Now I wonder what would please her,
Charlotte, Julia, or Louisa.
Ann and Mary, they're too common;
Joan's too formal for a woman;
Jane's a prettier name beside;
But we had a Jane that died.
They would say, if 'twas Rebecca,
That she was a little Quaker.
Edith's pretty, but that looks
Better in old English books;
Ellen's left off long ago;
Blanche is out of fashion now.

None that I have named as yet
Are so good as Margaret.
Emily is neat and fine.
What do you think of Caroline?
How I'm puzzled and perplexed
What to choose or think of next!
I am in a little fever.
Lest the name that I shall give her
Should disgrace her or defame her,
I will leave papa to name her.

Charles and Mary Lamb

*A Quaker is a particular sort of Christian. (It sounds as
if plenty of them were called Rebecca.)*

At Night

I'm frightened at night
When they put out the light
And the new moon is white.

It isn't so much
That I'm scared stiff to touch
The shadows, and clutch

My blankets: it's – oh –
Things long, long ago
That frighten me so.

If I don't move at all,
The moon will not fall,
There'll be no need to call.

But, strangely, next day
The moon slips away,
The shadows just play.

Elizabeth Jennings

Song

When I am dead, my dearest,
Sing no sad songs for me;
Plant thou no roses at my head,
Nor shady cypress tree:
Be the green grass above me
With showers and dewdrops wet;
And if thou wilt, remember,
And if thou wilt, forget.

I shall not see the shadow,
I shall not feel the rain;
I shall not hear the nightingale
Sing on, as if in pain;
And dreaming through the twilight
That doth not rise nor set,
Haply I may remember,
And haply may forget.

Christina Rossetti

'Haply' doesn't mean happily. It's an old-fashioned way
of saying 'perhaps'.

Overheard on a Saltmarsh

Nymph, nymph, what are your beads?

Green glass, goblin. Why do you stare at
them?

Give them me.

No.

Give them me. Give them me.

No.

Then I will howl all night in the reeds,
Lie in the mud and howl for them.

Goblin, why do you love them so?

They are better than stars or water,
Better than voices of winds that sing,
Better than any man's fair daughter,
Your green glass beads on a silver ring.

Hush, I stole them out of the moon.

Give me your beads, I want them.

No.

I will howl in a deep lagoon
For your green glass beads, I love them so.
Give them me. Give them me.

No.

Harold Monro

*A nymph is a water spirit. I think this poem works best
read out in two completely different voices – goblin and
nymph – even if you have to do both of them yourself.*

Look, Edwin!

Look, Edwin! Do you see that boy
Talking to the other boy?
No, over there by those two men –
Wait, don't look now – now look again.
No, not the one in navy-blue;
That's the one he's talking to.
Sure you see him? Stripèd pants?
Well, *he was born in Paris, France.*

Edna St Vincent Millay

*The line over the e in stripèd is an accent, telling you to
sound out the last half of the word as well, to keep the
rhythm straight. Say it both ways and you'll see that
works better.*

Where Go the Boats?

Dark brown is the river,
   Golden is the sand.
It flows along for ever,
   With trees on either hand.

Green leaves a-floating,
   Castles of the foam,
Boats of mine a-boating –
   Where will all come home?

On goes the river
   And out past the mill,
Away down the valley,
   Away down the hill.

Away down the river,
   A hundred miles or more,
Other little children
   Shall bring my boats ashore.

Robert Louis Stevenson

'There Was an Old Woman'

There was an old woman toss'd up in a basket
Seventeen times as high as the moon;
Where she was going I couldn't but ask it,
For in her hand she carried a broom.

Old woman, old woman, old woman, quoth I,
O whither, O whither, O whither, so high?
To brush the cobwebs out of the sky!
Shall I go with thee? *Ay, by-and-by.*

Traditional

*I don't know why I love this as much as I do, but, from
the first day I heard it, this has been my favourite
nursery rhyme.*

The Hippopotamus's Birthday

He has opened all his parcels
     but the largest and the last;
His hopes are at their highest
     and his heart is beating fast.
O happy Hippopotamus,
     what lovely gift is here?
He cuts the string. The world stands still.
     A pair of boots appear!

O little Hippopotamus,
     the sorrows of the small!
He dropped two tears to mingle
     with the flowing Senegal;
And the 'Thank you' that he uttered
     was the saddest ever heard
In the Senegambian jungle
     from the mouth of beast or bird.

E. V. Rieu

A Smuggler's Song

If you wake at midnight, and hear a horse's
      feet
Don't go drawing back the blind, or
      looking in the street,
Them that asks no questions isn't told a lie.
Watch the wall, my darling, while the
      Gentlemen go by!
    Five and twenty ponies
    Trotting through the dark –
    Brandy for the Parson,
    'Baccy for the Clerk;
    Laces for a lady, letters for a spy,
And watch the wall, my darling, while the
      Gentlemen go by!

Running round the woodlump if you
      chance to find
Little barrels, roped and tarred, all full of
      brandy-wine,
Don't you shout to come and look, nor use
      'em for your play.
Put the brushwood back again – and they'll
      be gone next day!

If you see the stable-door setting open wide;
If you see a tired horse lying down inside;
If your mother mends a coat cut about and
       tore;
If the lining's wet and warm – don't you
       ask no more!

If you meet King George's men, dressed in
       blue and red,
You be careful what you say, and mindful
       what is said.
If they call you 'pretty maid', and chuck
       you 'neath the chin,
Don't you tell where no one is, nor yet
       where no one's been!

Knocks and footsteps round the house –
       whistles after dark –
You've no call for running out till the
       house-dogs bark.
Trusty's here, and *Pincher*'s here, and see
       how dumb they lie –
They don't fret to follow when the
       Gentlemen go by!

If you do as you've been told, 'likely there's
      a chance,
You'll be give a dainty doll, all the way
      from France,
With a cap of Valenciennes, and a velvet
      hood –
A present from the Gentlemen, along o'
      being good!
    Five and twenty ponies
    Trotting through the dark –
    Brandy for the Parson,
    'Baccy for the Clerk.
Them that asks no questions isn't told a lie –
Watch the wall, my darling, while the
      Gentlemen go by!

Rudyard Kipling

*A Valenciennes cap is a lacy bonnet. After we read this,
we were set to write our own account of being a
smuggler's child. (No one suggested that this would be
anything other than fiction. But since even criminals'
children go to school, for some of us it may have been
closer to autobiography.)*

And So to Bed

'Night-night, my Precious!'; 'Sweet dreams,
  Sweet!'
'Heaven bless you, Child!' – the
  accustomed grown-ups said.
Two eyes gazed mutely back that none
  could meet,
Then turned to face Night's terrors overhead.

Walter de la Mare

*Interesting that no one wants to look him in the eye. The
grown-ups probably feel guilty because, deep inside, they
remember how scary it can be to lie alone upstairs.*

*And, just to show that these sorts of worries happen to
everyone, everywhere, here's another 'don't like being
alone in bed' poem.*

I Like to Stay Up

I like to stay up
and listen
when big people talking
jumbie stories

I does feel
so tingly and excited
inside me

But when my mother say
'Girl, time for bed'

Then is when
I does feel a dread

70

Then is when
I does jump into me bed

Then is when
I does cover up
from me feet to me head

Then is when
I does wish I didn't listen
to no stupid jumbie story

Then is when
I does wish I did read
me book instead.

Grace Nichols

Tartary

If I were Lord of Tartary,
  Myself, and me alone,
My bed should be of ivory,
  Of beaten gold my throne;
And in my court should peacocks flaunt,
And in my forests tigers haunt,
And in my pools great fishes slant
    Their fins athwart the sun.

If I were Lord of Tartary,
  Trumpeters every day
To all my meals should summon me,
  And in my courtyards bray;
And in the evening lamps should shine,
Yellow as honey, red as wine,
While harp, and flute, and mandoline
    Made music sweet and gay.

If I were Lord of Tartary,
　　I'd wear a robe of beads,
White, and gold, and green they'd be –
　　And small and thick as seeds;
And ere should wane the morning star,
I'd don my robe and scimitar,
And zebras seven should draw my car
　　　　Through Tartary's dark glades.

Lord of the fruits of Tartary,
　　Her rivers silver-pale!
Lord of the hills of Tartary,
　　Glen, thicket, wood, and dale!
Her flashing stars, her scented breeze,
Her trembling lakes, like foamless seas,
Her bird-delighting citron-trees,
　　　　In every purple vale.

Walter de la Mare

This next poem is a bit of a slog, if you want my opinion. But we hear it more and more because it's part of the American Christmas. You could try bullying an adult into reading you the whole thing, but you'd better choose one who will do it properly, or it'll be a very long time to be sitting politely, pretending to listen.

A Visit from St Nicholas

'Twas the night before Christmas, when all
   through the house
Not a creature was stirring, not even a mouse;
The stockings were hung by the chimney
   with care,
In hopes that St Nicholas soon would be
   there;
The children were nestled all snug in their
   beds,
While visions of sugar-plums danced in
   their heads;
And mamma in her 'kerchief, and I in my cap,
Had just settled our brains for a long
   winter's nap –
When out on the lawn there arose such a
   clatter,
I sprang from my bed to see what was the
   matter.
Away to the window I flew like a flash,
Tore open the shutters, and threw up the
   sash.

The moon, on the breast of the new-fallen
  snow,
Gave the lustre of midday to objects below;
When, what to my wondering eyes should
  appear,
But a miniature sleigh and eight tiny reindeer,
With a little old driver, so lively and quick,
I knew in a moment it must be St Nick.
More rapid than eagles his coursers they
  came,
And he whistled, and shouted, and called
  them by name:
'Now, *Dasher*! now, *Dancer*! now, *Prancer*
  and *Vixen*!
On, *Comet*! on, *Cupid*! on, *Donner* and *Blitzen*!
To the top of the porch! to the top of the wall!
Now dash away! dash away! dash away all!'
As dry leaves that before the wild
  hurricane fly,
When they meet with an obstacle, mount to
  the sky,
So up to the house-top the coursers they flew
With the sleigh full of toys, and St Nicholas
  too.

And then, in a twinkling, I heard on the roof
The prancing and pawing of each little hoof –
As I drew in my head, and was turning
  around,
Down the chimney St Nicholas came with a
  bound.
He was dressed all in fur, from his head to
  his foot,
And his clothes were all tarnished with
  ashes and soot;
A bundle of toys he had flung on his back,
And he looked like a pedlar just opening
  his pack.
His eyes – how they twinkled; his dimples,
  how merry!
His cheeks were like roses, his nose like a
  cherry!
His droll little mouth was drawn up like a
  bow,
And the beard of his chin was as white as
  the snow;
The stump of a pipe he held tight in his teeth,
And the smoke it encircled his head like a
  wreath;

He had a broad face and a little round belly
That shook, when he laughed, like a bowl
full of jelly.
He was chubby and plump, a right jolly old
elf,
And I laughed when I saw him, in spite of
myself;
A wink of his eye and a twist of his head
Soon gave me to know I had nothing to dread;
He spoke not a word, but went straight to
his work,
And filled all the stockings; then turned
with a jerk,
And laying his finger aside of his nose,
And giving a nod, up the chimney he rose;
He sprang to his sleigh, to his team gave a
whistle,
And away they all flew like the down of a
thistle.
But I heard him exclaim, ere he drove out
of sight,
'Happy Christmas to all, and to all a good night!'

Clement Clarke Moore

O Little Town of Bethlehem

O little town of Bethlehem
   How still we see thee lie!
Above thy deep and dreamless sleep
   The silent stars go by.
Yet in thy dark streets shineth
   The everlasting light;
The hopes and fears of all the years
   Are met in thee tonight.

O morning stars, together
   Proclaim the holy birth,
And praises sing to God the King,
   And peace to men on earth;
For Christ is born of Mary;
   And, gathered all above,
While mortals sleep, the angels keep
   Their watch of wondering love.

How silently, how silently,
  The wondrous gift is given!
So God imparts to human hearts
  The blessings of his heaven.
No ear may hear his coming;
  But in this world of sin,
Where meek souls will receive him, still
  The dear Christ enters in.

Where children pure and happy
  Pray to the blessèd Child,
Where misery cries out to thee,
  Son of the mother mild:
Where charity stands watching
  And faith holds wide the door,
The dark night wakes, the glory breaks,
  And Christmas comes once more.

O holy Child of Bethlehem,
   Descend to us, we pray;
Cast out our sin, and enter in,
   Be born in us today.
We hear the Christmas Angels
   The great glad tidings tell:
O come to us, abide with us,
Our Lord Emmanuel.

Bishop Phillips Brooks

The 'wondrous gift' in the third verse is the baby Jesus.
Emmanuel means 'God with us'.

Bobby Shaftoe

Bobby Shaftoe's gone to sea,
Silver buckles at his knee;
He'll come back and marry me,
  Bonny Bobby Shaftoe.

Bobby Shaftoe's bright and fair,
Combing down his yellow hair,
He's my ain for evermair,
  Bonny Bobby Shaftoe.

Bobby Shaftoe's tall and slim,
He's always dressed so neat and trim,
The ladies they all keek at him,
  Bonny Bobby Shaftoe.

Bobby Shaftoe's getten a bairn
For to dandle in his arm;
In his arm and on his knee,
  Bobby Shaftoe loves me.

Traditional

ain = own
keek = peek
bairn = baby

We have to hope that she's right and Bobby Shaftoe will be coming back, because clearly his baby is already on the way.

C is for Charms

I met a Strange Woman
With things in her arms.
'What have you got, Woman?'
'Charms,' she said, 'charms.

'I will put one on you
Ere I have done.
Which shall I put on you?'
'None,' I said, 'none!'

Oh how she smiled at me.
'Nay, then, my dear,
Look, do but look at them.
What do you fear?

'I've a black charm of night
And a gold one for noon,
A white charm for winter,
A rose charm for June;

'I've a green charm for woods,
And a blue charm for water,
And a silver for moons
When they're in their first quarter.

'I've a slow charm for growth,
And a swift one for birds,
And a soft one for sleep,
And a sweet one for words.

'I've a long charm of love,
And a strong charm for youth,
And one you can't change
Or destroy, for the truth.

'Sorry's the man, my dear,
Sorry,' she said,
'Who wanders through life
With no charm on his head.'

Oh how she smiled at me.
'Big one or small,
Which shall I put on you?'
'All,' I said, 'all!'

Eleanor Farjeon

The Walrus and
the Carpenter

The sun was shining on the sea,
    Shining with all his might:
He did his very best to make
    The billows smooth and bright –
And this was odd, because it was
    The middle of the night.

The moon was shining sulkily,
    Because she thought the sun
Had got no business to be there
    After the day was done –
'It's very rude of him,' she said,
    'To come and spoil the fun!'

The sea was wet as wet could be,
    The sands were dry as dry.
You could not see a cloud, because
    No cloud was in the sky:
No birds were flying overhead –
    There were no birds to fly.

The Walrus and the Carpenter
  Were walking close at hand;
They wept like anything to see
  Such quantities of sand:
'If this were only cleared away,'
  They said, 'it *would* be grand!'

'If seven maids with seven mops
  Swept it for half a year,
Do you suppose,' the Walrus said,
  'That they could get it clear?'
'I doubt it,' said the Carpenter,
  And shed a bitter tear.

'O Oysters, come and walk with us!'
  The Walrus did beseech.
'A pleasant walk, a pleasant talk,
  Along the briny beach:
We cannot do with more than four,
  To give a hand to each.'

The eldest Oyster looked at him,
    But never a word he said:
The eldest Oyster winked his eye,
    And shook his heavy head –
Meaning to say he did not choose
    To leave the oyster-bed.

But four young Oysters hurried up,
    All eager for the treat:
Their coats were brushed, their faces
    washed,
    Their shoes were clean and neat –
And this was odd, because, you know,
    They hadn't any feet.

Four other Oysters followed them,
    And yet another four;
And thick and fast they came at last,
    And more, and more, and more –
All hopping through the frothy waves,
    And scrambling to the shore.

The Walrus and the Carpenter
 Walked on a mile or so,
And then they rested on a rock
 Conveniently low:
And all the little Oysters stood
 And waited in a row.

'The time has come,' the Walrus said,
 'To talk of many things:
Of shoes – and ships – and sealing wax –
 Of cabbages – and kings –
And why the sea is boiling hot –
 And whether pigs have wings.'

'But wait a bit,' the Oysters cried,
 'Before we have our chat;
For some of us are out of breath,
 And all of us are fat!'
'No hurry!' said the Carpenter.
 They thanked him much for that.

'A loaf of bread,' the Walrus said,
  'Is what we chiefly need:
Pepper and vinegar besides
  Are very good indeed –
Now if you're ready, Oysters dear,
  We can begin to feed.'

'But not on us!' the Oysters cried,
  Turning a little blue.
'After such kindness, that would be
  A dismal thing to do!'
'The night is fine,' the Walrus said,
  'Do you admire the view?

'It was so kind of you to come!
  And you are very nice!'
The Carpenter said nothing but
  'Cut us another slice:
I wish you were not quite so deaf –
  I've had to ask you twice!'

'It seems a shame,' the Walrus said,
    'To play them such a trick,
After we've brought them out so far,
    And made them trot so quick!'
The Carpenter said nothing but
    'The butter's spread too thick!'

'I weep for you,' the Walrus said:
    'I deeply sympathize.'
With sobs and tears he sorted out
    Those of the largest size,
Holding his pocket-handkerchief
    Before his streaming eyes.

'O Oysters,' said the Carpenter,
    'You've had a pleasant run!
Shall we be trotting home again?'
    But answer came there none –
And this was scarcely odd, because
    They'd eaten every one.

Lewis Carroll

The Cheetah, My Dearest,
Is Known Not to Cheat

The cheetah, my dearest,
   is known not to cheat:
the Tiger possesses no tie;
The horse-fly, of course,
   was never a horse;
the lion will not tell a lie.

The turkey, though perky,
   was never a Turk;
nor the monkey ever a monk;
the mandrel, though like one,
   was never a man,
but some men are like him,
   when drunk.

The springbok, dear thing,
  was not born in the Spring;
The walrus will not build a wall.
No badger is bad; no adder can add.
There is no truth in these things at all.

George Barker

A mandrill is a large, hideous and ferocious monkey with
a bright red bottom.
  (I'm afraid George has spelt it wrong.)

The Land of Counterpane

When I was sick and lay a-bed,
I had two pillows at my head,
And all my toys beside me lay
To keep me happy all the day.

And sometimes for an hour or so
I watched my leaden soldiers go,
With different uniforms and drills,
Among the bed-clothes, through the hills;

And sometimes sent my ships in fleets
All up and down among the sheets;
Or brought my trees and houses out,
And planted cities all about.

I was the giant great and still
That sits upon the pillow-hill,
And sees before him, dale and plain,
The pleasant land of counterpane.

Robert Louis Stevenson

Ariel's Song
from *The Tempest*
(Act I, Scene ii)

Full fathom five thy father lies,
  Of his bones are coral made:
Those are pearls that were his eyes,
  Nothing of him that doth fade,
But doth suffer a sea-change
Into something rich and strange:
Sea-nymphs hourly ring his knell –
  Hark! now I hear them,
    Ding-dong bell.

William Shakespeare

*The spirit Ariel sings this to Prince Ferdinand after a
magical shipwreck. It isn't true. His father didn't drown.
But Ariel is right that changes are about to happen.*

*In class, after reading this, we all had to write a letter
to someone, telling the most frightful lie. I can't recall
exactly what I invented, but I remember I really enjoyed
writing it.*

This next poem is about William the Conqueror.

William sailed from Normandy (part of France) and conquered England at the Battle of Hastings in 1066, when King Harold died from an arrow in his eye.

The Seine is a river in France. The Inn of the Four Ways lies at a crossroads.

But what the poet's saying is that, given William came from such a gorgeous country, and could have had such a pleasant, easy life, why on earth did he bother?

Norman William

Had I been Norman William,
With orchards such as these,
With fields so green and flowery,
With such tall poplar trees;
And with the bright broad Seine
Curling through hill and plain,
The thought of Harold's England would
                  have tempted me in vain.

Had I been Norman William
Possessing for my goods
Fairytale thatched cottages
And fairy-haunted woods,
I would have passed my days
Afar from battle frays,
Drinking sweet apple cider at the Inn of the
                  Four Ways.

Eleanor Farjeon

The Tree and the Pool

'I don't want my leaves to drop,' said the tree.
'I don't want to freeze,' said the pool.
'I don't want to smile,' said the sombre man.
'Or ever to cry,' said the Fool.

'I don't want to open,' said the bud.
'I don't want to end,' said the night.
'I don't want to rise,' said the neap-tide.
'Or ever to fall,' said the kite.

They wished and they murmured and
    whispered,
They said that to change was a crime.
Then a voice from nowhere answered,
'You must do what I say,' said Time.

Brian Patten

sombre = glum; neap-tide = lowest tide
I expect you don't fancy growing old. But 'You must do what I say,' says Time. If you were to write something under the title 'Myself at Eighty', how do you suppose it would go?

'Monday's child'

Monday's child is fair of face,
　　Tuesday's child is full of grace,
Wednesday's child is full of woe,
　　Thursday's child has far to go,
Friday's child is loving and giving,
　　Saturday's child works hard for its living,
And the child that is born on the Sabbath day
　　Is bonny and blithe, and good and gay.

Traditional

*Sooner or later, reading this rhyme, everyone wants to
find out which sort of child they are. If your parents
can't remember, you can always ask your librarian. They
have ways of finding out everything.*

This next poem, by Tennyson, tells of the terrible event which took place in 1854 in the Crimea (now Ukraine) at Balaclava (where winters were so cold that those woolly face helmets were first used).

The Light Brigade (who ride into battle on smaller, faster horses than the Heavy Brigade) courageously followed the order to charge, but, because of a misunderstanding, it was towards the wrong guns.

In twenty minutes, 247 men were killed or wounded, and almost all the horses died.

The Charge of the Light Brigade

Half a league, half a league,
   Half a league onward,
All in the valley of Death
   Rode the six hundred.
'Forward the Light Brigade!
Charge for the guns!' he said;
Into the valley of Death
   Rode the six hundred.

'Forward the Light Brigade!'
Was there a man dismay'd?
Not tho' the soldier knew
   Someone had blunder'd:
Theirs not to make reply,
Theirs not to reason why,
Theirs but to do and die:
Into the valley of Death
   Rode the six hundred.

Cannon to right of them,
Cannon to left of them,
Cannon in front of them
  Volley'd and thunder'd;
Storm'd at with shot and shell,
Boldly they rode and well,
Into the jaws of Death
Into the mouth of Hell
  Rode the six hundred.

Flash'd all their sabres bare,
Flash'd as they turn'd in air,
Sabring the gunners there,
Charging an army, while
  All the world wonder'd:
Plunged in the battery-smoke
Right thro' the line they broke;
Cossack and Russian
Reel'd from the sabre-stroke
  Shatter'd and sunder'd.
Then they rode back, but not,
  Not the six hundred.

Cannon to right of them,
Cannon to left of them,
Cannon behind them
   Volley'd and thunder'd;
Storm'd at with shot and shell,
While horse and hero fell,
They that had fought so well
Came thro' the jaws of Death,
Back from the mouth of Hell,
All that was left of them,
   Left of six hundred.

When can their glory fade?
O the wild charge they made!
   All the world wonder'd.
Honour the charge they made!
Honour the Light Brigade,
   Noble six hundred!

Alfred, Lord Tennyson

All Things Bright
and Beautiful

All things bright and beautiful,
    All creatures great and small,
All things wise and wonderful,
    The Lord God made them all.

Each little flower that opens,
    Each little bird that sings,
He made their glowing colours,
    He made their tiny wings.

The purple-headed mountain,
    The river running by,
The sunset, and the morning,
    That brightens up the sky;

The cold wind in the winter,
  The pleasant summer sun,
The ripe fruits in the garden,
  He made them every one.

He gave us eyes to see them,
  And lips that we might tell,
How great is God Almighty,
  Who has made all things well.

Cecil Francis Alexander

This is what we call the original. Now read the next poem.

All Things Dull and Ugly

All things dull and ugly,
All creatures short and squat,
All things rude and nasty,
The Lord God made the lot.

Each little snake that poisons,
Each little wasp that stings,
He made their brutish venom,
He made their horrid wings.

All things sick and cancerous,
All evil great and small,
All things foul and dangerous,
The Lord God made them all.

Each nasty little hornet,
Each beastly little squid.
Who made the spikey urchin?
Who made the sharks? He did.

All things scabbed and ulcerous,
All pox both great and small,
Putrid, foul and gangrenous,
The Lord God made them all.

Eric Idle

This is what we call the spoof, or parody.

The Way Through
the Woods

They shut the road through the woods
Seventy years ago.
Weather and rain have undone it again,
And now you would never know
There was once a road through the woods
Before they planted the trees.
It is underneath the coppice and heath,
And the thin anemones.
Only the keeper sees
That, where the ring-dove broods,
And the badgers roll at ease,
There was once a road through the woods.

Yet, if you enter the woods
Of a summer evening late,
When the night-air cools on the trout-
   ringed pools
Where the otter whistles his mate
(They fear not men in the woods,
Because they see so few),
You will hear the beat of a horse's feet,
And the swish of a skirt in the dew,
Steadily cantering through
The misty solitudes,
As though they perfectly knew
The old lost road through the woods . . .
But there is no road through the woods!

Rudyard Kipling

from *The Glass Slipper*

Cinderella sings as she lays and lights the fire:

I wish plates didn't get greasy,
I wish stockings didn't get holes,
And sweeping and scouring and
    scrubbing were easy,
I wish
There weren't coals.

I wish bells didn't keep ringing,
And tablecloths never got tears,
Or stoves wanted blacking or beans
    wanted stringing,
I wish
There weren't stairs.

I wish meals didn't want laying,
I wish they ate out of a dish,
I wish there was more time for laughing
   and playing,
I wish . . .
I wish . . .

Eleanor Farjeon

*One of my daughters wrote her own version of this
poem. She had a far cushier life than any scullery maid
but the poem still came out a mile long. I suppose
everyone has their own grumbles. You might want to see
how long your version would end up . . .*

Memento Mori

He died
we buried him
his first rain fell tonight

Sabahattin Kudret Aksal
(trans. Feyyaz Kayacan Fergar)

Memento Mori *is Latin and stands for 'a reminder of*
death'. (People sometimes kept a skull on their desks, as a
memento mori.)

But this poem is really about how, after someone dies,
you can't just switch to a different way of thinking about
them. It's a wonderful example of how a very few words
can say so much.

Stopping by Woods
on a Snowy Evening

Whose woods these are I think I know.
His house is in the village, though;
He will not see me stopping here
To watch his woods fill up with snow.

My little horse must think it queer
To stop without a farmhouse near
Between the woods and frozen lake
The darkest evening of the year.

He gives his harness bells a shake
To ask if there is some mistake.
The only other sound's the sweep
Of easy wind and downy flake.

The woods are lovely, dark and deep,
But I have promises to keep,
And miles to go before I sleep,
And miles to go before I sleep.

Robert Frost

At school, we were forever having to learn poems, then stand on the stage to recite them. I think I became practically allergic to this next one. I reckon no one can say it aloud without sounding half self-pitying and half self-important. (But you could have a go to try and prove me wrong.)

'Break, Break, Break'

Break, break, break
    On thy cold grey stones, O Sea!
And I would that my tongue could utter
    The thoughts that arise in me.

O well for the fisherman's boy,
    That he shouts with his sister at play!
O well for the sailor lad,
    That he sings in his boat on the bay!

And the stately ships go on
    To their haven under the hill;
But O for the touch of a vanish'd hand
    And the sound of a voice that is still!

Break, break, break,
    At the foot of thy crags, O Sea!
But the tender grace of a day that is dead
    Will never come back to me.

Alfred, Lord Tennyson

'Oranges and Lemons'

'Oranges and lemons,'
Say the bells of Saint Clement's,
'You owe me five farthings,'
Say the bells of Saint Martin's.
'When will you pay me?'
Say the bells of Old Bailey.
'When I grow rich,'
Say the bells of Shoreditch.
'Pray when will that be?'
Say the bells of Stepney.
'I'm sure I don't know,'
Says the great bell of Bow.
'Brickbats and tiles,'
Say the bells of Saint Giles.
'Old Father Baldpate,'
Say the slow bells at Aldgate.
'Pokers and tongs,'
Say the bells of Saint John's.

'Kettles and pans,'
Say the bells of Saint Anne's.
'Pancakes and fritters,'
Say the bells of Saint Peter's.
'Two sticks and an apple,'
Say the bells of Whitechapel.
Here comes the candle to light you to bed.
And here comes the chopper to chop off
   your HEAD.

Traditional

*Words, like church bell chimes, have their inner
rhythms. Here, the beginning chimes of different London
churches are tricked out as words.*

*In years of plague, the bells can hardly ever have been
silent. In class, we wrote our own diaries of the Black
Death, and pretty gruesome they were, too.*

This creepy little number is more than 250 years old. It showed up in the earliest book of English nursery rhymes, Tommy Thumb's Pretty Song Book, *in 1744.*

The Death and Burial of Cock Robin

Who killed Cock Robin?
  I, said the Sparrow,
  With my bow and arrow,
I killed Cock Robin.

Who saw him die?
  I, said the Fly,
  With my little eye,
I saw him die.

Who caught his blood?
  I, said the Fish,
  With my little dish,
I caught his blood.

Who'll make his shroud?
  I, said the Beetle,
  With my thread and needle,
I'll make the shroud.

Who'll dig his grave?
  I, said the Owl,
  With my pick and shovel,
I'll dig his grave.

Who'll be the parson?
  I, said the Rook,
  With my little book,
I'll be the parson.

Who'll be the clerk?
  I, said the Lark.
  If it's not in the dark,
I'll be the clerk.

Who'll carry the link?
　I, said the Linnet,
　I'll fetch it in a minute,
I'll carry the link.

Who'll be chief mourner?
　I, said the Dove,
　I mourn for my love,
I'll be chief mourner.

Who'll carry the coffin?
　I, said the Kite,
　If it's not through the night,
I'll carry the coffin.

Who'll bear the pall?
　We, said the Wren,
　Both the cock and the hen,
We'll bear the pall.

Who'll sing a psalm?
  I, said the Thrush,
    As she sat on a bush,
I'll sing a psalm.

Who'll toll the bell?
  I, said the Bull,
    Because I can pull,
So Cock Robin, farewell.

All the birds of the air
  Fell a-sighing and a-sobbing,
When they heard the bell toll
  For poor Cock Robin.

Traditional

Someone once pointed out to me that, when you look out of a train or car window, what's close rushes past you in one direction, what's in the middle distance seems to stay fairly still, and what's on the far horizon gradually moves along the other way entirely, turning the view into a sort of oddly spinning plate.

Up until then, I hadn't noticed. And I rather suspect that Robert Louis Stevenson didn't either.

From a Railway Carriage

Faster than fairies, faster than witches,
Bridges and houses, hedges and ditches;
And charging along like troops in a battle,
All through the meadows the horses and
  cattle:
All the sights of the hill and the plain
Fly as thick as driving rain;
And ever again, in the wink of an eye,
Painted stations whistle by.

Here is a child who clambers and scrambles,
All by himself and gathering brambles;
Here is a tramp who stands and gazes;
And there is the green for stringing the
  daisies!
Here is a cart run away in the road
Lumping along with man and load;
And there is a mill and there is a river:
Each a glimpse and gone forever!

Robert Louis Stevenson

Little Orphant Annie

Little Orphant Annie's come to our house
  to stay,
An' wash the cups and saucers up,
  an' brush the crumbs away,
An' shoo the chickens off the porch,
  an' dust the hearth, an' sweep.
An' make the fire, an' bake the bread,
  an' earn her board-an'-keep.
An' all us other children, when the
  supper things is done,
We set around the kitchen fire
  an' has the mostest fun
A-list'nin to the witch-tales
  'at Annie tells about,
An' the Gobble-uns 'at gits you
        Ef you
              Don't
                  Watch
                      Out!

Onc't there was a little boy wouldn't say
   his pray'rs –
An' when he went to bed at night,
   away up stairs,
His mammy heerd him holler,
   an' his daddy heerd him bawl,
An' when they turn't the kivvers down,
   he wasn't there at all!
An' they seeked him in the rafter-room,
   an' cubby-hole, an' press,
An' seeked him up the chimbly-flue,
   an' ever'wheres, I guess;
But all they ever found was thist his pants
   an' roundabout!
An' the Gobble-uns'll git you
      Ef you
         Don't
           Watch
              Out!

An' one time a little girl 'ud allus laugh
   an' grin,
An' make fun of Ever' one,
   an' all her blood-an'-kin;
An' onc't when they was 'company',
   an' ole folks was there,
She mocked 'em an' shocked 'em,
   an' said she didn't care!
An' thist as she kicked her heels,
   an' turn't to run an' hide,
They was two great big Black Things
   a-standin' by her side,
An' they snatched her through the ceilin'
   'fore she knowed what she's about!
An' the Gobble-uns'll git you
      Ef you
         Don't
            Watch
               Out!

An' little Orphant Annie says,
  when the blaze is blue,
An' the lampwick sputters,
  an' the wind goes woo-oo!
An' you hear the crickets quit,
  an' the moon is grey,
An' the lightnin'-bugs in dew is
  all squenched away, –
You better mind yer parents,
  and yer teachers fond and dear,
An' churish them 'at loves you,
  an' dry the orphant's tear,
An' he'p the pore an' needy ones
  'at clusters all about,
Er the Gobble-uns'll git you
       Ef you
           Don't
               Watch
                   Out!

James Whitcomb Riley

The Rag Doll to the Heedless Child

I love you
with my linen heart.

You cannot
know how these

rigid, lumpy arms
shudder in your grasp,

or what
tears dam up against

these blue eye-smudges at
your capriciousness.

At night I watch you sleep;
you'll never know

how I thrust my face
into the stream

of your warm breath;
and how

love-words choke me behind
this sewn-up mouth.

David Harsent

*It's bad enough having to make sure you take proper care
of your pets. If all your soft toys had as strong feelings as
this doll, I doubt if you'd ever have found the time to be
reading this.*

The Spare Room

It was just the spare room
the nobody-there room
the spooks-in-the-air room
the unbearable spare room.

It wasn't the guest room
the four-poster best room
the designed-to-impress room
the unusable guest room.

It wasn't the main room
the homely and plain room
the flop-on-the-bed room
Mum and Dad's own room.

It wasn't the blue room
the sweet lulla-loo room
the creep-on-your-feet room
the baby's asleep room.

It wasn't the bright room
the clothes-everywhere room
the music-all-night room
sister's scattered-about room.

It was just the spare room
the nobody-there room
the spooks-in-the-air room
the unbearable spare room.

Diana Hendry

*Now that most of us have central heating and televisions
and computers, very few people have an unused spare
room.*

*But you'll still come across them in older people's
houses.*

My Sister Clarissa Spits
Twice if I Kiss Her

My sister Clarissa spits twice if I kiss her
and once if I hold her hand.
I reprimand her – my name's Alexander –
for spitting I simply can't stand.

'Clarissa, Clarissa, my sister, is this a
really nice habit to practise?'
But she always replies with innocent eyes
rather softly, 'Dear Brother, the fact is

I think I'm an ape with a very small grape
crushed to juice in my mastodon lips.
Since I am not a prude, though I hate being
  rude,
I am simply ejecting the pips.'

George Barker

Lullaby of an Infant Chief

O hush thee, my baby, thy sire was a knight,
Thy mother a lady, both lovely and bright;
The woods and the glens, from the towers
   which we see,
They all are belonging, dear baby, to thee.

O fear not the bugle, though loudly it blows,
It calls but the warders that guard thy repose;
Their bows would be bended, their blades
   would be red,
Ere the step of a foeman drew near to thy bed.

O hush thee, my baby, the time soon will come,
When thy sleep shall be broken by trumpet
   and drum;
Then hush thee, my darling, take rest while
   you may,
For strife comes with manhood, and
   waking with day.

Sir Walter Scott

Repose is rest or sleep.

The Key of the Kingdom

This is the key of the kingdom:
In that kingdom is a city,
In that city is a town,
In that town there is a street,
In that street there winds a lane,
In that lane there is a yard,
In that yard there is a house,
In that house there waits a room,
In that room there is a bed,
On that bed there is a basket,
   A basket of flowers.

Flowers in the basket,
Basket on the bed,
Bed in the chamber,
Chamber in the house,
House in the weedy yard,
Yard in the winding lane,
Lane in the broad street,
Street in the high town,
Town in the city,
City in the kingdom:
    This is the key of the kingdom.

Traditional

I used to adore this sort of wind-in-and-wind-out rhyme.
They always seemed to me like one of those old-fashioned
films that start with the camera swooping down on one
particular house in a small town, and then, after the
happy ending, drawing back out again.

I think this next poem is really good advice for letter-writing.

Indite, here, just means to get down in words.

Young Children used to practise their written work on wipeable slates.

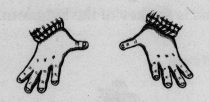

How to Write a Letter

Maria intended a letter to write,
But could not begin (as she thought) to indite;
So went to her mother with pencil and slate,
Containing 'Dear Sister', and also a date.

'With nothing to say, my dear girl, do not
      think
Of wasting your time over paper and ink;
But certainly this is an excellent way,
To try with your slate to find something to
      say.

'I will give you a rule,' said her mother, 'my
      dear,
Just think for a moment your sister is here,
And what would you tell her? Consider,
      and then,
Though silent your tongue, you can speak
      with your pen.'

Elizabeth Turner

Jabberwocky

'Twas brillig, and the slithy toves
   Did gyre and gimble in the wabe;
All mimsy were the borogoves,
   And the mome raths outgrabe.

'Beware the Jabberwock, my son!
   The jaws that bite, the claws that catch!
Beware the Jubjub bird, and shun
   The frumious Bandersnatch!'

He took his vorpal sword in hand:
   Long time the manxome foe he sought –
So rested he by the Tumtum tree,
   And stood awhile in thought.

And as in uffish thought he stood,
   The Jabberwock, with eyes of flame,
Came whiffling through the tulgey wood,
   And burbled as it came!

One, two! One, two! And through and
    through
  The vorpal blade went snicker-snack!
He left it dead, and with its head
  He went galumphing back.

'And thou hast slain the Jabberwock?
  Come to my arms, my beamish boy!
O frabjous day! Callooh! Callay!'
  He chortled in his joy.

'Twas brillig, and the slithy toves
  Did gyre and gimble in the wabe;
All mimsy were the borogoves,
  And the mome raths outgrabe.

Lewis Carroll

*I hope you'll be able to track down Sir Arthur Tenniel's
brilliant illustration of the Jabberwock in Lewis Carroll's
book about Alice,* Through the Looking Glass.

Windy Nights

Whenever the moon and stars are set,
    Whenever the wind is high,
All night long in the dark and wet,
    A man goes riding by.
Late in the night when the fires are out,
Why does he gallop and gallop about?

Whenever the trees are crying aloud,
    And ships are tossed at sea,
By, on the highway, low and loud,
    By at the gallop goes he.
By at the gallop he goes, and then
By he comes back at the gallop again.

Robert Louis Stevenson

*This is a poem about how, when you're alone in bed,
noises you hear can make your imagination run wild.
Or is it?*

Morning

Will there really be a morning?
　　Is there such a thing as day?
Could I see it from the mountains
　　If I were as tall as they?
Has it feet like water lilies?
　　Has it feathers like a bird?
Is it brought from famous countries
　　Of which I've never heard?
Oh, some scholar! Oh, some sailor!
　　Oh, some wise man from the skies!
Please to tell a little pilgrim
　　Where the place called morning lies.

Emily Dickinson

Index of Titles/First Lines

Index of Poets

Acknowledgements

The publishers and the compiler thank the following for permission to reprint copyright material:

John Agard, 'Mouth Open, Story Jump Out' from *Say It Again Granny* (The Bodley Head, 1986), copyright © John Agard, 1986; reprinted by permission of The Random House Group Ltd.

Sabahattin Kudret Aksal, 'Memento Mori' from *Modern Turkish Poetry*, edited and translated by Feyyaz Kayacan Fergar (Rockingham Press, 1992), copyright © the Estate of Feyyaz Fergar, 1992; reprinted by permission of the Rockingham Press.

George Barker, '"My Heart Is Broken," Cried the Owl', 'My Sister Clarissa Spits Twice if I Kiss Her' and 'She Lies by the Island of Spices and Zephyrs' from *To Aylsham Fair* (Faber and Faber, 1970), copyright © George Barker, 1970; 'The Cheetah, My Dearest Is Known Not to Cheat' from *Runes and Rhymes* (Faber and Faber, 1969), copyright © George Barker, 1969; reprinted by permission of Faber and Faber Ltd.

Hilaire Belloc, *'Child, do not throw this book about'* and 'The Yak' from *Complete Verse* (Pimlico, 1991), copyright © the Estate of Hilaire Belloc, 1970; reprinted by permission of Peters, Fraser and Dunlop Ltd on behalf of the Estate of Hilaire Belloc.

Charles Causley, 'The Reverend Sabine Baring-Gould' from *Selected Poems for Children* (Macmillan, 1997), copyright © Charles Causley, 1997; reprinted by permission of David Higham Associates on behalf of the author.

Debjani Chatterjee, 'My Sari' from *Unzip Your Lips: 100 Poems to Read Aloud* (Macmillan Children's Books, 1998), copyright © Dr Debjani Chatterjee, 1998; reprinted by permission of the author.

Leonard Clark, 'Fog in November' from *Four Seasons* (Dobson Books Ltd, 1975), copyright © Leonard Clark, 1975; reprinted by permission of the Literary Executor of Leonard Clark.

E. E. Cummings, 'Hist Whist' from *Complete Poems 1904–62*, edited by George J. Firmage, copyright © the Trustees for the E. E. Cummings Trust and George James Firmage, 1991; reprinted by permission of W. W. Norton and Company.

Neil Curry, 'The Doll's House' from *Ships in Bottles* (Enitharmon Press, 1988), copyright © Neil Curry, 1988; reprinted by permission of Enitharmon Press.

Walter de la Mare, 'The Listeners', 'The Song of Shadows', 'And So to

of the Authors Licensing and Collecting Society on behalf of the Estate of the late E. V. Rieu.

Kit Wright, 'The Magic Box' from *Cat Among the Pigeons* (Viking Kestrel, 1987), copyright © Kit Wright, 1987; reprinted by permission of the author.

Every effort has been made to trace the copyright holders of poems included in this anthology, but in some cases this has not proved possible. The publishers therefore wish to thank the authors or copyright holders of those poems which are included without acknowledgement above. The publishers would be grateful to be notified of any errors or omissions in the above list and will be happy to make good any such errors or omissions in future printings.